Breakthrough Communication Skills

Speak with Confidence and Clarity

Table of Contents

Chapter 1. Introduction

Welcome to our Special Report on "Breakthrough Communication Skills: Speak with Confidence and Clarity"! In this comprehensive compilation, we demystify the art of communication and inject it with a level of simplicity and excitement that's sure to inspire change. This is far from the realm of technical jargon, but a stimulating journey that will transform how you interact with the world around you. Your speaking ability is about to take an extraordinary leap forward. Are you ready to infuse your conversations with authenticity, poise, and unmistakable clarity? Dive in and discover the power of confident communication waiting to be unlocked within you. With this report by your side, you won't just talk - you'll electrify!

Chapter 2. Mastering the Art of Verbal Expressions

If there's one art that stands at the intersection of human interaction, it's verbal expression. How we choose to articulate our thoughts and feelings greatly influences the impression we leave on others. Let's take a deep dive into the mastery of this important communication skill.

2.1. Understanding Verbal Expression

Verbal expression is the capability to convey thoughts, ideas, or emotions using language. It's more than merely speaking words; it's about effective storytelling, engagement, and impact. Understanding the core elements of verbal expression involves recognizing the purpose of communication, understanding your listener's perspective, and awarely utilizing elements of language to accomplish your communication goals.

Let's think about communication as an equation:

```
Verbal Expression = (Purpose of Communication +
Understanding of Listener) x Language Usage
```

When all these components come together effectively, the result is successful verbal expression.

2.2. The Purpose of Communication

Understanding the purpose of your communication is the starting foundation of effective verbal expression. Every time you converse, whether in a casual conversation, a meeting, a presentation, or a talk, you're fulfilling a purpose.

This purpose could be:

1. Informing: Sharing information or data with others.

2. Persuading: Trying to convince someone to accept your point of view.

3. Instructing: Teaching someone to do something.

4. Entertaining: Telling a story or joke to delight or amuse.

2.3. Understanding Your Listener

Knowing your audience is an essential aspect of effective communication. Taking your listener's perspective ensures you adjust your message to their knowledge level, interest, and receptivity. Are they experts in your topic, or do they have no background information? Are they receptive or resistant to your message? The answers to these questions can shape the way you craft your verbal expressions.

2.4. The Language Element

Language brings ideas to life. The words you choose create imagery, convey emotions, and can either simplify or complicate the ideas you want to share. They leave an impression in the listener's mind and influence their responses. Therefore, choosing the right words is critically pivotal in verbal expression.

2.5. Perfecting Verbal Expression

Now that we understand what constitutes verbal expression, how do we channel it correctly?

2.6. The Role of Clarity

Clarity stands as the cornerstone of verbal communication. Avoid using complex language or jargon, unless necessary. Simplicity leads to understanding, which is the ultimate goal of any communication. Ambiguity often leads to misunderstanding and subsequently, communication breakdown.

2.7. Emote to Evoke

Emotion is the universal language. By injecting emotion into your verbal expressions, you can connect with listeners on a deeper level. Use emotional ask, and you'll note how much more engaged they are.

2.8. Storytelling: The Super Glue of Engagement

Humans are wired to enjoy and remember stories. Transforming your point into a compelling story can significantly increase the impact of your message. It also makes your message stand out among the flood of information that people receive daily.

2.9. Active Listening: The Hidden Element

While speaking, always ensure you also practice active listening. It involves receiving, understanding, and providing an empathic response to the speaker's message. It allows you to understand your listeners and refine your message on the go, enhancing communicative effectiveness.

2.10. The Power of Tone and Pace

How you sound—your tone and pace—convey just as much meaning as your words. Using the right tone can enhance understanding and influence how your message is perceived. Similarly, the pace of your speech can help to build suspense or emphasize key points.

2.11. The Marriage of Verbal and Nonverbal

Even though our focus is on verbal expressions, nonverbal cues are equally crucial in achieving impactful communication. Your body language, facial expressions, and gestures must align with your verbal communication.

2.12. Conclusion

Becoming a master of verbal expression isn't an overnight process. It requires practice, reflection, and a willingness to learn and adjust based on feedback. As we've discovered, the way to effectively communicate isn't just about what you say - it's about understanding your purpose and listener, choosing appropriate language, maintaining clarity, displaying authentic emotion, crafting engaging stories, listening actively, controlling your tone and pace, and aligning your verbal output with non-verbal cues. Engage with these steps intentionally, and soon, you'll be an expert communicator, ready to express your thoughts, ideas, and emotions with confidence and clarity.

Chapter 3. Body Language: Speaking Without Words

Before a single word leaves your lips, you have already started communicating. Through the art of body language, you've said more than you may realize. Let's dive into this wordless dialogue that shapes so much of human interaction.

3.1. Understanding Body Language

Body language, also known as kinesics, refers to the non-verbal signals that we use in communication. From facial expressions, posture, and even the space we keep between ourselves and others, each movement and gesture tells a story. They express our mood, attitudes, and emotions, often more convincingly than our spoken words.

It's often overlooked, but it's estimated that up to 55% of our communication occurs through these subtle, non-verbal cues. To have a full command over your communicative abilities, it is critical to be skilled both in expressing yourself and understanding these cues in others.

3.2. The Key Components of Body Language

Consider body language as a language of its own, with its vocabulary and grammar. Let's break down these components to better decode this visual dialect.

1. **Facial Expressions**: They hold the capacity for a vast array of emotions. By picking up on smiles, frowns, furrowed brows, or widened eyes, we can infer an assortment of feelings - happiness,

anger, surprise, worry, and more.

2. **Posture and Body Movements**: The way we sit, stand, and move communicates volumes about our comfort, confidence, attentiveness, or territoriality.

3. **Gestures**: These include our numerous hand movements, nods, or shakes that can convey agreement, disagreement, emphasis, or thoughtfulness.

4. **Eye Contact**: This maintains connection and indicates interest or intensity.

5. **Space and Proximity**: How close we stand or sit near others symbolizes our relationship and engagement.

6. **Touch**: When, how, and whom we touch illustrates levels of intimacy or imposition.

3.3. Reading and Interpreting Body Language

Body language plays a significant role in how our messages are received and interpreted. To be effective in our communication, we need to understand both the language of our body and the body language of others. Your goal is to ensure your body and words align harmoniously, radiating authenticity.

Our brains instinctively assess and interpret body language. However, it's crucial not to jump to conclusions about what others' gestures might mean. Take into account the overall context, including the words being used, the tone of voice, the situation, the culture, and past behaviors. Pay special attention to repeated patterns in body language as these are more likely to be accurate.

3.4. Mastering Your Own Body Language

Integrating thoughtful body language can magnify your communicative prowess. Here are some techniques to harness this silent vocabulary:

1. **Align your Body Language with your Words**: Synchronize your verbal and non-verbal communication. If you speak about something positive, ensure your body expresses openness and relaxation.

2. **Utilize Mirroring**: Reflect the body language of the person you are interacting with subtly. This builds rapport and shows empathy.

3. **Mind your Posture**: Stand and sit upright, which directly shows confidence and authority, besides being beneficial for your physical health.

4. **Eye Contact**: Maintain it appropriately. Too much can feel confrontational; too little can seem dismissive or shy.

5. **Control your Expressions**: Smile when it's appropriate, show attentiveness and interest, and regulate your negative expressions.

6. **Use Gestures Strategically**: This adds dynamism to your communication and helps emphasize key points.

3.5. Cultivating Emotional Intelligence

Understanding body language transcends communication—it can bolster your emotional intelligence. Emotional intelligence is your ability to understand and manage your and others' emotions. With improved interpretation of body language, you garner insight into hidden emotions, enabling better decisions and interactions.

3.6. The Pitfalls of Misinterpretation

Body language doesn't operate in a vacuum—it varies from person to person and culture to culture, and is influenced by context. Therefore, avoid making absolute judgments based on a single gesture. Consider the complete picture, observing clusters of cues to interpret the overall message.

3.7. In Conclusion

Body language, this silent orchestra of nods, expressions, postures, and eye contact, reflects our true sentiments. In grasping its secrets, you'll discover tools that will not only enhance your communication, but also your understanding of yourself and others. Remember, the essence of body language is the same as verbal communication: to share and understand thoughts, feelings, and intentions. Once you've mastered these techniques, you'll realize that you're not just speaking, but communicating in its purest form.

The path to mastering body language is a journey of constant learning, adaptation, and observation. Keep an open mind, be receptive, and embrace the communicative beauty of what remains unsaid. And above all, remember to practice—it's not always what you say, it's how you say it.

Chapter 4. Speaking with Clarity: How to Remove Ambiguity

Clarity in communication is vital to being understood. When your words are clear, your intent is easy to discern and misunderstandings are conveniently avoided. This clarity can only emerge when you decide to shed ambiguity from your communication, whether oral or written.

4.1. Determining the Purpose of Your Message

The first step toward clarity is understanding the purpose of your message. What do you wish to accomplish with your words? Do you want to inform, persuade, instruct, or entertain?

Before crafting your message, take some time to determine its intent. This understanding will guide you in choosing the right words and format for your content. It will also help you identify and eliminate any potential areas of ambiguity ahead of time, ensuring your message hits its mark with precision.

4.2. Formulating Your Thoughts

Before verbalizing your thoughts, take a moment to formulate them in your mind. This can greatly reduce the chances of ambiguity in your speech. Organize your thoughts logically and sequentially. It may be helpful to visualize your sentences, and the relationships between them, to ensure their clarity. Practicing or rehearsing beforehand can give you a sense of the flow and progression of your thoughts.

4.3. Clear and Simple Words

A significant portion of clarity relies on your choice of words. While it might be tempting to show off your expansive vocabulary, this does not necessarily translate into effective communication. Simple, widely understood words are often the best when it comes to clear communication. The goal is to be understood, not to cause confusion. Save the ornate language for poetry—in everyday communication, the simplest words are the most powerful.

4.4. Sensitivity to Your Audience

Exercising a sense of audience awareness is a crucial part to achieving clarity. What are their ages, educational backgrounds, areas of interest, cultural contexts? All these factors can influence how well they understand your message.

Being sensitive to your audience's needs and understanding can prevent ambiguity in your speech. Adapt your language, tone, and style to what your audience can easily connect with and understand. This might mean using technical jargon only when speaking with a more specialized audience, or incorporating analogies and examples when explaining a complex concept to a novice.

4.5. Maintaining Logical Flow

A good message has a beginning, a middle, and an end. It has a logical flow to it. Clarity is achieved when ideas move smoothly from one to the next. The transition between thoughts should be seamless, creating a coherent and comprehensive message.

To achieve this, be organized in your presentation of the content. You can use cue words or phrases to guide transitions ("Keeping this in mind, let's now move on…", "In contrast,…", "Furthermore,…") which prevent confusion and maintain logical progression.

4.6. Being Specific

Another facet of clarity is specificity. Ambiguity often stems from being too general or vague. Instead, focus on being explicit, using details to paint a clear picture of your message.

This isn't about verbosity, but rather precision. It's about choosing the right descriptive words, using concrete examples, providing clear definitions where needed, and answering questions such as "Who?", "What?", "When?", "Where?", "Why?", and "How?" when relevant.

Complicated ideas are easier to grasp when broken down into specific, manageable parts. So avoid generalities and dig into the details, ensuring that your information is understood.

4.7. Active Listening

While it might seem strange to include listening in a discussion about speaking, it plays a critical role in clear communication. Active listening is the practice of fully focusing on, understanding, responding to, and remembering what the other person is saying.

To ensure clarity, use active listening when the roles are reversed and you're the listener. This is an opportunity to ask clarifying questions or paraphrase the speaker's points for your own understanding. This confirms that you get the message right and demonstrates good communication etiquette to the other person, hopefully inspiring them to do the same when you're speaking.

4.8. Body Language

Communication isn't just about the words you speak. Your body language has a role in how your message is received and interpreted. Pay attention to your gestures, posture, eye contact, and facial expressions as they should be consistent with the message you are delivering.

When your body language does not match the message, it creates ambiguity. A speaker seeming uncomfortable or nervous can lead to the message being diluted or misunderstood.

In sum, speaking with clarity is a skill that can be honed with time and practice. Ensure you understand the purpose of your message, keep your words simple, maintain a logical flow, and listen actively. And don't forget to use body language to your advantage. With these strategies, you can confidently communicate with clarity, making ambiguity a thing of the past. Your words will resonate with their intended purpose and meaning, ensuring that your message is understood by all.

Chapter 5. Confidence: The Hidden Secret of Great Communicators

There's an underlying secret weapon every great communicator wields effortlessly yet powerfully. That weapon: boundless confidence. Unwrapping this secret means navigating a fascinating journey of self-discovery, enhanced awareness, and transformative mindsets. Let's drive straight into this riveting exploration.

Understanding Confidence ===

Confidence, in its essence, is self-assuredness; it's a conviction in one's own abilities. It's the distinct, powerful feeling that you are capable, competent, and can face the challenges that life throws at you. But it's more than just a feeling. Confidence is a compass guiding you through your interactions with others, helping you to present yourself and your ideas more clearly and convincingly.

Unwrapping the Confidence Conundrum ===

So how does confidence influence communication? In truth, confidence is the silent echo behind every effective communicator's voice. Confidence has the ability to validate and strengthen the message you're trying to send. It gives weight to your words, persuading your audience to listen, understand, and act upon them.

Confidence makes your message clearer. It aids in establishing a quick and strong connection with your audience, reduces misunderstandings, and increases the chance of your message getting across as intended.

Developing Inspiring Confidence ===

The phrase "fake it till you make it" can often be misguided when it comes to cultivating authentic confidence. True confidence doesn't spring from inauthenticity or mimicry but from understanding, embracing, and developing your skills and capabilities. Here's how you can set about doing just that.

Self-awareness --- Knowing yourself, your motivations, strengths, and weaknesses is the first step towards building genuine confidence. Self-awareness makes you cognizant of how you react to situations, helping you to control your reactions and feelings better. Not to mention, recognizing and accepting your strengths cultivates a positive self-perception, subsequently leading to higher confidence.

Practice and Preparedness --- Confidence grows with familiarity and mastery. The more you practice your communication - be it public speaking, negotiations, or daily conversations - the more confident you become in your abilities to get your point across effectively. Preparing well for your interactions, understanding your content thoroughly, and anticipating possible audience reactions can significantly bolster your confidence.

Positive Mindset --- Adopting a positive mindset goes a long way towards building a confident persona. The way you think about yourself directly impacts your self-confidence. Encourage positive self-talk, believe in your abilities, and remember your past successes when faced with challenging situations. Remember, a confident communicator is not someone who never fails but someone who never gives up.

Embrace Failure as a Learning Opportunity --- Everyone, at some point, faces communication failures. What differentiates confident communicators is how they interpret these situations. They see them as learning opportunities rather than dead-ends. By investigating what went wrong, developing an improvement plan, and encouraging oneself to try again, failures become stepping stones to success.

Fear, The Confidence Killer and How to Overcome It ===

Perhaps the biggest barrier to confident communication is fear: fear of rejection, of making a mistake, or of not being good enough. Fear takes hold of our thoughts and actions, hindering our ability to communicate effectively.

But here's the trick. Confident people also experience fear; they've just mastered the art of dealing with it. The solution is not to eliminate fear but to manage and harness it. Recognize that fear is a natural reaction, an indicator that something matters to you. Then channel that energy toward improving your performance instead of eroding your confidence.

A practical approach is to practice your communication in front of a friendly audience or in a low-stakes environment first and gradually work your way up, thereby training your mind to manage fear and perform well despite it.

Embody Confidence: A Powerful Non-Verbal Communication Tool ===

Non-verbal cues often speak louder than words. The way you dress, carry yourself, make eye contact, and control your voice pitch and body language can either regulate or contradict the words you say. Therefore, it is vital to present an image that radiates confidence.

Master Eye Contact --- Maintaining appropriate eye contact communicates confidence and interest in your listeners. It also helps you to gauge their reactions and adapt your communication accordingly.

Adopt a Confident Posture --- Stand tall, open your shoulders, and keep your head up. This posture not only signals confidence to your audience but also boosts your own feeling of self-assuredness.

Hearty Handshake --- A firm but not overly strong handshake can effectively communicate your confidence and professionalism before you even utter a word.

Dress for Success --- The way you dress and groom yourself can considerably influence your perceived confidence. Dressing appropriately for any given situation improves your self-image and, consequently, enhances your confidence.

Incorporate Powerful Gestures --- Use body language to emphasize your verbal communication. Gestures should be natural and relevant to your speech. Open hand gestures, nodding, and mirroring your audience's movements are some strategies to enhance connection and portray confidence.

The Dance of Confidence and Humility ===

While confidence is necessary, it's essential to dodge the pitfall of overconfidence which can come across as arrogance. Striking the balance between confidence and humility is a delicate dance that requires self-awareness and introspective honesty.

Remember, humility doesn't mean downplaying or undervaluing your competence or accomplishments. It entails recognizing your capabilities genuinely and acknowledging that there is always room for growth and improvement. Stay open to feedback and make an effort to learn continually, thereby ensuring that your confidence never crosses over into arrogance.

With these insights, embark on the journey of cultivating your confidence. As you do, you'll find that the effects are transformative, not just on your communication skills, but on your overall personal and professional life. Embrace the challenges, remain resilient through the setbacks, and soon, you'll be communicating with assurance, authenticity, and irresistible charm that electrifies.

Chapter 6. Active Listening: A Critical Component of Communication

The relationship between communication and active listening is much like the bond between two sides of a coin - inseparable and complementary. Active listening goes beyond just hearing what the other person is saying. It involves understanding, interpreting, and reacting to the message conveyed. This might sound like an effortless process, but it has a profound influence on the quality of your communication. As one embarks on the journey to mastering this essential skill, the overarching aim is to build meaningful connections, foster understanding, and promote enriching, clear conversations.

6.1. How Active is Your Listening?

We've all heard the adage - God gave us one mouth and two ears, so we should listen twice as much as we speak. How true is this in your life? Communication isn't merely about expressing your ideas eloquently or having a stunning vocabulary. It also includes a crucial skill - active listening. Before delving into how to cultivate this skill, it's necessary to understand what it means.

Active listening is a technique that involves fully concentrating, understanding, responding, and then remembering what's being said in a conversation. It's not a passive activity but an active, engaging, and rewarding process.

6.2. The Art of Active Listening

Breaking down active listening, we find two significant ingredients —

attention and response. When combined, these lead to a holistic understanding of the conversation at hand. It can be broken down further into five interactive components:

1. Understanding: Grasping the complete meaning of the sender's message.

2. Interpretation: Deciphering the sender's exact intentions.

3. Evaluation: Analyzing the message without letting personal bias interfere.

4. Remembering: Retaining crucial parts of the conversation.

5. Response: Providing feedback using verbal or non-verbal cues.

These five components are not part of a linear process. Instead, they work together and overlap, leading to the dynamic phenomenon of active listening.

6.3. Active Listening Versus Passive Listening

Active and passive listening exist at opposite ends of the listening spectrum. Passive listening involves just hearing the speaker without any engagement or understanding, whereas, in active listening, the listener thoroughly engages in the interaction and processes the information consciously.

Passive listening can be compared to watching a movie without concentrating on the plot; you might catch sporadic parts of the conversation but not fully understand the storyline. Conversely, active listening means fully engaging with the dialogue, processing it, and creating personalized feedback or responses.

6.4. Building Blocks of Active Listening

Active listening can be broken down into different building blocks or sets of skills, each vital to the process:

1. Attending: This involves showing constructive, non-verbal signals demonstrating that you are engaged in the conversation.

2. Responding: A critical component where the listener provides verbal responses to show their engagement and understanding.

3. Clarifying: When uncertain, the listener should seek clarification to avoid misinterpretation.

4. Reflecting: The listener makes an effort to reflect on the speaker's sentiments to show empathy.

Active listening isn't purely an auditory process; it combines verbal and non-verbal cues to truly connect with the speaker's message.

6.5. Strategies to Enhance Active Listening

If active listening seems like a difficult task, fear not! Here are some strategies that can help improve it:

1. Stay Present: Keep distractions at bay and focus solely on the speaker.

2. Be Patient: Give time to the speaker without interrupting.

3. Showcase Interest: Avoid daydreaming and show genuine interest.

4. Reflect: Paraphrasing an important point shows you are processing the dialogue.

5. Clarification: Rather than assume, ask questions.

6. Feedback: Provide constructive feedback on the conversation.

By adhering to these strategies, you stimulate an environment where each party feels heard, understood, and valued, thereby enhancing the quality of interactions.

Active listening is a vital communication skill, acting as the bedrock for any successful conversation. It involves being present, understanding, interpreting, evaluating, retaining, and responding to the conversation. This seemingly simple technique can transform how effectively you communicate. Remember, it's not just about hearing; but essentially, about understanding. The journey towards mastering active listening may seem daunting at first, but with time and practice, it will become second nature, transforming the way you communicate and ultimately, how you connect with the world around you.

Chapter 7. Harnessing the Power of Emotional Intelligence

Regardless of the communication skills one might master, connecting on a deeper, more emotional level with your interlocutor will always add an exceptional quality to your conversations. This captivating world we're about to embark on is the world of emotional intelligence. Experts in the field believe emotional intelligence or EQ (Emotional Quotient) might even surpass IQ in terms of its importance in our personal and career success.

So, how does one cultivate and harness this power? It starts by understanding its core pillars, which are self-awareness, self-management, social awareness, and relationship management.

7.1. Self-Awareness: The Power Within

Self-awareness is the foundation upon which every other aspect of emotional intelligence is based. It refers to your ability to identify your emotions and understand their impact on your thoughts, decisions, and behavior. It's about consciously knowing what you're good at while acknowledging what you still have yet to learn - about clarifying your values yet understanding where they came from.

While self-awareness is a term often thrown out lightly, gaining it is far from trivial. It takes in-depth self-reflection, candid feedback, and a commitment to growth. Consider keeping a journal where you record your emotions and how they impact your actions. Or, seek honest feedback from friends and colleagues on how they perceive you.

Understanding yourself offers you remarkable control over your interactions. When you can pinpoint your emotional reactions, you can begin to manage them, leading us to the next pillar.

7.2. Self-Management: Acquiring Emotional Agility

Self-management transcends self-control. It's about harnessing your emotions and using them to fuel progress, development, and positive change. It means exhibiting flexibility in adapting your emotions and responses to various situations.

To foster emotional agility, it's vital to practice mindfulness, which basically means living in the present. In a conversation, focus on your communication partner, their words, their body language, instead of being preoccupied by your thoughts and potential responses. Exhibit an ongoing commitment to honesty, integrity, and ethical responsibility.

Remember what Dwight D. Eisenhower once said: "You do not lead by hitting people over the head—that's assault, not leadership." Leadership is about consistency, reliability, and trustworthiness - all factors dependent on effective self-management.

7.3. Social Awareness: Sensing the Unspoken

While the first two pillars address our relationship with ourselves, social awareness involves understanding others and the emotions they exhibit. This often means comprehending what isn't being directly communicated: the unspoken words, restrained feelings, or hidden messages conveyed through nonverbal cues.

To hone this ability, you must foster an attitude of curiosity and empathy. Listen more than you speak, and try to decode the underlying messages. Occasionally paraphrasing what you've understood gives the speaker assurance that their message is being received and understood. Practice active engagement in conversations.

Putting yourself in another person's shoes isn't an easy task, but with patience, you will improve.

7.4. Relationship Management: The Art of Connection

Contrary to what you might think, effective relationship management builds upon all of the previous aspects. Combining self and social awareness, applying self-management, you can effectively manage your relationships—be it with teammates, colleagues, friends, or family.

To illustrate how interactions can be framed, let's consider the SCARF model by David Rock, which explains that our concerns in social interactions are often based around Status, Certainty, Autonomy, Relatedness, and Fairness (SCARF).

Develop an awareness of how a person may feel threatened or rewarded in these areas, and communicate accordingly. Also, practice assertiveness, conflict resolution, team capability building, and inspirational leadership.

Lastly, remember that emotional intelligence is not a trait you either do or do not possess. It is a set of skills—a mental muscle that can be trained and toned with consistent practice. So, start today. The transformation will be worthwhile.

Chapter 8. Communication and Leadership: The Inextricable Link

Abruptly, the hue and cry of the room dies when you enter. Eyes turn towards you, hearts pound slightly faster, and for a momentary pause, the cloak of silence envelops the space. As you take your position at the helm, there's a visible synchronization of breathing, an unspoken anticipation lingering in the air. It isn't fear or dread that holds your audience captive - it's respect, it's attention, it's anticipation, it's a mark of great leadership. This scene paints a familiar portrait of leaders across the board - be it in politics, business, or social settings - and one sterling quality that seizes the spotlight is their communication skill.

Indeed, communication serves as the lifeblood in the remarkable synthesis of leadership. Recognizing this undeniable link acts as the bedrock for successful leadership practices.

8.1. The Core of Leadership: Effective Communication

Effective communication breathes life into leadership. As a leader, your words should not just speak but sing - with clarity, conviction, and a profound connection with your audience. Leaders must be storytellers, strategic negotiators, keen listeners, and inspirational orators all rolled into one. Engulfed by the challenges of an fast-paced globalized world, leaders are required to master the chorus and symphony of communication to effectively navigate their teams.

It's a tale as old as time that every great leader is also an accomplished communicator. Be it Martin Luther King Jr. or Steve

Jobs, their communication prowess redefined levels of influence and persuasion, creating an enduring legacy. Distilling their hallmark strategies, we can ascertain that clarity of vision, precision in articulation, and emotional resonance form the cornerstone of potent communication.

Leaders also need to be adept at multi-channel communication, navigating different forms with ease - verbal, non-verbal, and written. By harnessing these channels, leaders can shape a compelling narrative that resonates with every stakeholder, be it a team member, a customer, or a business partner.

8.2. The Dual Aspects of Communication in Leadership: Transmission and Reception

Communication is not a one-way street. Instead, it's a two-lane highway connecting transmission and reception. Successful leaders understand this balance and exercise their abilities to convey their thoughts (transmission) while understanding others' perspectives effectively (reception).

Transmission goes beyond delivering a message. It's a complex process of framing thoughts, giving them the embrace of appropriate words, and delivering them with the right tone and body language to ensure understanding. Successful leaders are not just clear communicators, but also effectively modulate their style depending on their audience.

Reception, on the other hand, involves being a good listener. A leader must encourage dialogues over monologues, fostering an atmosphere of inclusion and openness. Active listening is an integral component of this process. It implies understanding, interpreting and reacting appropriately to a message.

Building bridges and not walls with communication empowers your team, fosters innovation, betters problem-solving and, ultimately, steers your organization to achieve your collective vision.

8.3. The Role of Empathy in Leadership Communication

At the heart of effective communication lies empathy, a trait that endows a leader with the ability to understand and share the feelings of others. Empathy fuels deeper connections, builds trust, and sparks collaboration—making it an indispensable attribute for leaders.

Leaders who demonstrate empathy validate their team's thoughts and emotions, nurturing a culture of understanding. This empathy can extend to crafting messages that meet their team's emotional and psychological needs, which in turn fosters motivation and commitment.

For leaders, the saying 'actions speak louder than words' rings particularly true. Demonstrating empathy through action—one that corresponds with your communicated message—reinforces the authenticity of your leadership. Being congruent in your words and deeds increases your trustworthiness, one of the hallmarks of effective leadership communication.

8.4. The Power of Feedback: A Leadership Communication Knack

Feedback forms an essential part of the communication matrix in leadership. Constructive feedback aids in personal development, improves performance, and motivates team members. Done effectively, it serves as a potent tool for change, fostering a culture of continuous learning and improvement.

Feedback can be a two-way street. Leaders should encourage feedback from their team members, as it lends fresh perspectives and enables them to make better decisions. By inviting feedback, leaders also convey their respect for the team's opinions, thus strengthening their connection with them.

Effective communication is a cornerstone of leadership. Whether it's articulating a vision, empathetically engaging with team members, or providing and receiving feedback, leaders must not only focus on what they communicate but also how they do. With effort, practice, and awareness, leaders can harness the power of communication to inspire, shepherde and drive performance.

This chapter has aimed to illuminate the inextricable link between communication and leadership, underscoring the importance of nurturing this critical skill. Now, as you rewrite your leadership journey, remember every word you utter, every gesture you make and every feedback you give or take is an opportunity. An opportunity to inspire, to connect, to lead.

Chapter 9. Understanding and Overcoming Communication Barriers

To effectively harness your communication skills, a fundamental first step is understanding the barriers that disrupt the process of communication, and how to effectively overcome them. This course is not about eliminating these barriers altogether - a Sisyphean task - but rather, navigating within or around them to enhance the clarity and authenticity of your communication.

9.1. Fear and Anxiety: Mental Blockades That Bind Us

One of the most potent barriers to effective communication is fear. Many people have an ingrained fear of public speaking, expressing their opinions, or simply being misunderstood. This fear could stem from a lack of confidence, past negative experiences, or the dreaded thought of failure and rejection.

Anxiety, too, plays a pivotal role in hampering communication. It manifests in physical symptoms - an increase in heart rate, tremors, excessive sweating, and even dry mouth. Such anxiousness not only affects your ability to express thoughts, but can also create a negative impression on the listener.

To overcome these mental barriers, it's essential to practice mindfulness. Recognize your fear and anxiety triggers and approach them with acceptance rather than avoidance. A good way to begin is slowly exposing yourself to the situations that cause fear or anxiety and gradually building resilience through repeated practice.

Public speaking clubs, such as Toastmasters International, or even regular presentations in a safe, supportive environment can help you adapt to such situations. Employing relaxation techniques, like deep breathing and progressive muscle relaxation, can also alleviate symptoms of anxiety.

9.2. Language Differences: The Linguistic Tightrope

Language differences present another major hurdle in communication. Not all individuals might understand or be proficient in the language you're using to communicate. Even within a single language, dialects and accents can pose challenges.

There are multiple solutions to overcoming this barrier. First, it's about understanding your audience. If you're communicating with non-native speakers, it would be beneficial to use simple language, avoid jargon, and speak slowly and clearly.

Learning the basics of other languages could prove useful, especially in multilingual environments. Taking advantage of translation and language learning tools, like Google Translate or DuoLingo, can make this task easier.

9.3. Physical Environment: The Neglected Barrier

The physical environment may seem like an insignificant factor affecting communication, but it can have a surprisingly significant impact. Noisy surroundings, poor lighting, or even uncomfortable seating arrangements can pose distractions that deter effective communication.

To combat this, put thought into where and when you communicate.

Opt for quiet and comfortable environments whenever possible. For challenging or serious conversations, physical comfort can help maintain focus and ease tension.

9.4. Non-Verbal Communication: Unspoken Words That Speak Volumes

Up to 93% of communication is non-verbal, including body language, facial expressions, and even tone of voice. Non-verbal cues greatly influence how our message is interpreted.

To enhance your non-verbal communication, be mindful of your body language, maintain eye contact, and modulate your pitch and tone based on the situation. Consider your audience's non-verbal cues to understand their feelings and responses.

9.5. Technological Barriers: The Downside of a Digital Age

While technology provides numerous avenues for communication, it introduces its own set of barriers. Misunderstandings can occur due to poor network connections, missing non-verbal cues in text-based communication, or the impersonal nature of digital communication.

Overcoming technological barriers involves ensuring a stable internet connection, using video calls to retain visual cues, and incorporating empathy and personal-touch in digital communication.

9.6. Constraints of Time and Attention

In today's fast-paced world, people often find they lack the time or attention to communicate effectively. Rushed communication can result in misunderstandings and misinterpretations.

Planning and designating specific time for important conversations can help overcome this barrier. Practicing active listening and mindfulness improves attention during communication.

Understanding and overcoming these barriers can revolutionize your communication skills. By putting these strategies into practice, you will not just break down the walls that have confined your communication skills; you'll construct bridges for more genuine and clearer connections.

Chapter 10. Powerful Persuasion: Influencing Through Communication

Persuasion is both an art and a science, rooted deeply in our ability to communicate effectively. While many assume persuasion to be exclusive to salespeople and negotiators, the reality is that we are all involved in some form of persuasion almost every day. Whether you're convincing your kids to eat their vegetables, coaxing your team to follow through on an idea, or encouraging a friend to try out a new experience, persuasion is at play.

However, it's not about commanding or manipulating others. True persuasion is about influence through sincere communication, understanding the other person's perspective, and presenting your ideas in a manner that appeals and resonates with them. Ultimately, becoming a powerful persuader is about harnessing the ability to positively impact those around you.

10.1. Unraveling the Power of Words

Words have power. They can repair a broken relationship, ignite a revolutionary idea, or reassure a scared child. When used effectively, words can be instrumental in persuading others. To begin with, make your language direct, clear, and straightforward. Omit ambiguous or complex jargon that may confuse your listeners. You want your audience to have a firm grasp of your message, not be lost in a cluster of intricate terms.

Using visual language can also enhance your persuasive impact. Words that provoke mental images can stimulate a listener's imagination, hence encouraging a more personal and profound connection with the speaker's point of view. For instance, instead of saying "our profit has increased significantly," you might say "our profit has shot up like a rocket." The latter conjures a more vivid illustration of the situation, creating a stronger impact.

Lastly, remember the influence of apt metaphors and analogies. They can help break down complex concepts into understandable chunks, thereby improving comprehension and receptiveness to your ideas.

10.2. Harnessing Non-Verbal Communication

Communication is not limited to words. Non-verbal communication - our body language, tone of voice, and facial expressions - often conveys more than we could express through words. In fact, according to the renowned psychologist, Dr. Albert Mehrabian, only 7% of our communication consists of the literal content of the message. The use of voice, like tone and inflection, accounts for 38%, while body language stands at a whopping 55%.

To enhance your persuasive impact, ensure your non-verbal communication aligns with your spoken message. For example, if you're trying to express enthusiasm about a project, let that excitement bubble through your tone and physical demeanor. Lean in while speaking, vary your pitch and pace to emphasize important points, use animated facial expressions, and maintain an open posture. All these cues send unspoken messages of your commitment and passion.

10.3. Building Rapport

Establishing a connection with your audience is a crucial component of persuasive communication. We tend to be more influenced by those we like or identify with. This is where the skill of building rapport becomes invaluable. Genuine interest in the other person, active listening, empathy, and mirroring body language are effective ways to build rapport and mutual trust.

Remember, rapport-building isn't about creating a fake persona; instead, it's about finding common ground, displaying understanding, and treating others with respect during interactions.

10.4. Mastering the Art of Storytelling

Storytelling is arguably one of the most powerful tools for persuasion. It engages your listeners on an emotional level, making your message more memorable and influential. Through stories, you can inspire, challenge, provoke thought, and ignite change.

When crafting your story, ensure it has a clear and compelling narrative. Draw on personal experiences or relevant scenarios to underscore your point. Interest and emotion are the cornerstones of a great story. So, involve your own emotions, and aim to reach the emotions of your listeners to make your story more relatable and impactful.

Beyond words, stories need a rhythm. Build a flow, steadily rising towards a climax, then ensuring a brief period for digesting the takeaways before you proceed with the conversation.

10.5. Constructive Dialogue

Idea exchange forms the basis of persuasion. More than just presenting your thoughts, engaging your audience in a dialogue allows them to contribute, raising the chance they'll be receptive to your point of view.

Practice active listening - giving undivided attention to the speaker, summarizing their thoughts for clarification, and providing thoughtful responses. This not only signals respect for their ideas but also provides valuable insights into their concerns, allowing you to tailor your message for better resonance.

10.6. Call to Action

Every persuasive conversation should end with a compelling call to action. Now that you've depicted a clear picture, tell your audience what step they need to take next. Be clear, concise, and ensure the action is related directly to the conversation you had. A well-crafted call to action leaves your audience with a sense of direction, compelling them to move towards the change you are championing.

In conclusion, the art of persuasion is a mastery of effective communication. It's a blend of clear language, compelling body language, empathetic connection, engaging storytelling, constructive dialogue, and a compelling call to action. With consistent practice and mindful application of these techniques, your everyday interactions will be transformed, and your persuasive impact will be undeniable.

Chapter 11. Creating Impact: Your Strategic Communication Blueprint

Communication, at its core, is about transmitting ideas, thoughts, and emotions from one entity to another. The success of communication is not just measured by the mere act of sharing an idea, but the ability to elicit a desired response or action from the receiver. This particular prowess, the ability to create impact through communication, is what sets exceptional communicators apart. In this carefully curated discourse, we delve into strategic communication, the blueprint that seals the deal between talking and making a lasting impact.

The foundation of impactful communication is understanding the basic elements that make it up. It consists of the sender, the message and the receiver, with the feedback loop completing the circle. Yet in this simplicity, a complexity emerges. The art lies in crafting the message in a way that not just appeals to the receiver, but motivates them to act or change.

11.1. Understanding the Fundamentals

There are three key aspects to creating impact through communication – clarity, confidence, and authenticity.

Clarity is the precision and understandability of your message. It's about crafting your message in such a way that it cannot be misunderstood, it remains clear of ambiguities, and lands as intended.

Confidence, on the other hand, imbues your message with authority and credibility. It's the component that ensures your message is given the weight it deserves. Confidence also aids in maintaining poise during challenging or high-pressure scenarios.

Lastly, authenticity is about being real, genuine, and honest in your communication. It's about connecting on an emotional level and showcasing vulnerability, which helps build meaningful and relatable conversations.

Let's dissect these dimensions further:

11.2. Clarity in Communication

Clarity in communication begins with understanding your audience, knowing what message you want to deliver to them, and developing a clear strategy of how you're going to accomplish that. Here's a breakdown of how you can accomplish this:

1. Identify your audience: Know their backgrounds, beliefs, sensitivities, likes, and dislikes. It's crucial to frame your message in a way that aligns with the listener's perspectives.

2. Know your message: What are you trying to communicate? Ensure you understand it fully before conveying it to others. If it is complex, break it down into simpler, digestible parts.

3. Create a strategy: How will you deliver your message? Would a story work better or should you stick to facts and figures? The nature of your message and the receivers' profile should determine the approach.

11.3. Confidence: The Assertive Influence

Confidence is often misunderstood as being loud or dominant. In fact, it's the polar opposite. It is about communicating assertively, with respect and empathy for others. Here are ways you can instill confidence in your communication:

1. Self-authenticity: Being your genuine self breeds self-confidence. Embrace your uniqueness and let it radiate in your conversation.

2. Knowledge: Understand your subject matter inside out. It is easier to communicate confidently when you know what you're talking about.

3. Listen Actively: Good communication isn't just about talking, but listening as well. If you listen attentively, you can respond more confidently.

11.4. Authenticity: The Emotional Connection

Authenticity in communication fuels connection and promotes trust. It makes your message more relatable and effective. Here are some approaches to incorporate authenticity:

1. Embrace vulnerability: It's okay to accept that you don't know everything. It makes you human and fosters closeness.

2. Stay true to your values: Don't change your stance just to please your audience. Stand by your beliefs and let them shape your message.

3. Show empathy: Understand others' feelings and perspectives, and communicate with care. It attracts emotional investment from the audience.

11.5. Creating your Blueprint

Constructing your strategic communication blueprint involves combining these three aspects effectively. Start with the groundwork, by understanding your audience and context. Progress to moulding your message with clarity, delivering it with confidence, and keeping authenticity at the forefront to truly connect with your audience.

1. Analyze: Start by understanding your audience's needs, potential response patterns, and the overall context.

2. Draft: Create a tangible embodiment of your message; iterate over it to improve clarity and avoid ambiguity.

3. Deliver: Use assertiveness and poise to convey your message with authority, and remember, confidence is not dominance but respect for other's views.

4. Evolve: Continually assess feedback and refine your communication blueprint. Be ready to adapt and change according to situation and audience.

Remember, the power to create a lasting impact lies in strategic, effective communication. Clarity ensures your message is understood in its intended form. Confidence gives weight to your words and adds to your credibility. Authenticity invites trust, making your message resonate. Embrace this triad, and you are well on your way to being a communicator who leaves an indelible imprint.